HISTORIC PHOTOS OF
HARRY S. TRUMAN

TEXT AND CAPTIONS BY LARRY JOHNSON

TURNER
PUBLISHING COMPANY
Nashville, Tennessee   Paducah, Kentucky

Truman signs county checks with a multiple pen in 1927. Under his eight-year administration as county judge (equivalent to county commissioner), he oversaw the construction of high-quality roads and public buildings. He was so frugal during the construction of a new courthouse, he had enough funds to commission statues of his hero, Andrew Jackson.

HISTORIC PHOTOS OF
HARRY S. TRUMAN

Turner Publishing Company
200 4th Avenue North • Suite 950   412 Broadway • P.O. Box 3101
Nashville, Tennessee 37219   Paducah, Kentucky 42002-3101
(615) 255-2665   (270) 443-0121

www.turnerpublishing.com

Historic Photos of Harry S Truman

Library of Congress Control Number: 2007933771

ISBN-13: 978-1-59652-403-3

Printed in the United States of America

07 08 09 10 11 12 13 14—0 9 8 7 6 5 4 3 2 1

CONTENTS

After his return from France, Truman joined the Reserves. At the annual summer exercises, Truman made several important political acquaintances like Dwight P. Griswold. Seen here in uniform with Truman, Griswold would later become governor of Nebraska and play a role in Truman's postwar administration.

Acknowledgments

This volume, *Historic Photos of Harry S. Truman,* is the result of the cooperation and efforts of many individuals and organizations. It is with great thanks that we acknowledge in particular the valuable contribution of the Truman Presidential Museum and Library.

Pamela Bracken provided inestimable assistance in editing and proofreading.

The author would also like to thank Margaret Nell, whose schoolgirl crush on Harry S. Truman was a great inspiration.

PREFACE

It is often said that Harry S. Truman was the least prepared man ever to become President of the United States. He had not graduated from a university. He had not conducted any brilliant military campaigns. He had not come from a wealthy family. He had not built a successful business. He had not even forged his character during a difficult life of poverty.

One could say, however, that Truman spent a lifetime preparing, however unknowingly, to step into the rather large shoes of Franklin D. Roosevelt. Harry S. Truman was a student of history. He had read history almost since he could read at all and his diaries and letters indicate he frequently drew inspiration and guidance from its pages. He was keenly aware of history—and that he was making it.

From his parents Truman learned the value of hard work and the strength of strong morals and devotion to duty. Throughout his life he listened to that inner voice, a true moral compass, which enabled him to endure his delayed start in adult life, sustained him during his fierce campaigns, helped him remain calm as the world unraveled after the war, and gave him the courage to act decisively as in the use of the atomic bomb and his ambitious civil rights program. He also accepted responsibility for those actions when he famously said, "The buck stops here!"

Truman also learned early the value and rich rewards of human interaction. Despite living a childhood in relative isolation, his early adulthood was spent building social networks. Whether it be business clubs, the Masons, or the military, Truman made loyal friends and powerful allies. Here he learned to listen and to lead.

The photographs presented in this collection richly illustrate the life of Harry S. Truman, one of the least complex and most transparent of our presidents. He was not particularly image-conscious—he cared little what others thought of him—but he always dressed impeccably and smiled when he found the camera. Because of the valuable, standard-setting work of the Truman Presidential Library and Museum in making his diaries and letters available, as well as oral histories and the photographs themselves, we have been able to illuminate the photographs even further. By salting them with facts and quotations about the events and subjects depicted, Truman's life and career come alive on the book's pages.

A number of excellent works exist on the subject of Harry S. Truman and his presidency. This book does not pretend to be a political biography or to provide analysis of his life or career. Indeed, through the use of newspaper accounts, interviews, and diary entries, the captions have a contemporaneous feel that is intended to place one in the milieu of the photograph. That this is an immensely entertaining book is due in large part to Harry S. Truman himself and his knack for what we would today call "sound bites." As he said, "I never give them hell. I just tell the truth and they think it's hell."

Harry, Margaret, and Bess stand with Rear Admiral Monroe Kelly during the christening and launching of the USS *Missouri* on January 29, 1944. The "Mighty Mo" was a ship of superlatives and fought with distinction in the Pacific Theater. Her greatest fame came as she hosted the surrender of Japan on September 2, 1945.

LEARNING

(1884–1918)

Harry S. Truman was born to Martha Ellen and John Anderson Truman in the family home in Lamar, Missouri, on May 8, 1884. John Truman moved the family (later joined by a son, John Vivian, and daughter, Mary Jane) to several towns in western Missouri before agreeing to manage his wife's family farm in Grandview in 1887. He did well.

Harry lived on this farm surrounded by a large extended family. He marveled at the tales his grandmother would tell of the blue-jacketed devils who ravaged their farm and those of so many of their neighbors during the Civil War. From his grandfather he learned of life in the Wild West. But it was Harry's mother who made sure there were plenty of books in the home and taught him to read them. It was then that Harry's poor eyesight was discovered and he was fitted with a pair of expensive glasses.

In 1890, Mamma Truman decided Harry needed better schooling and the family moved to Independence, Missouri. Harry later recalled an idyllic childhood there. His glasses, bookishness, and frequent music lessons did not make him popular, but he had a few close friends, including his two cousins Nellie and Ethel Noland.

Throughout his school years in Independence, a particular girl caught his eye—one Elizabeth Wallace, scion of a prominent family in town. He was too shy to court her in high school, but he did see her often at her neighbors, the Nolands. After graduation in 1901, they would not see each other for several years.

After high school, Harry entered a wandering period in his life. Unable to attend West Point because of poor eyesight, he lacked the means to attend another college. He worked at several jobs in Kansas City but found no direction there. Finally, in 1906, after his family had returned to Grandview, his father summoned him to come help; Harry dutifully obeyed.

Harry worked hard on the farm for the next ten years, but he wanted more. He joined the National Guard. He began to court Bess, making the arduous trip into Independence several nights a week and writing when he didn't. After his father died in 1914, he also made a number of ill-fated investments in oil, land, and minerals.

It was in his artillery service during World War I that Harry unknowingly found his place. He found he could be a leader of men and that he had a knack for remaining calm and focused under fire. His correspondence with Bess carried him through those frightful days of combat and he married her weeks after he returned home.

Harry's parents Martha Ellen Young and John Anderson Truman on their wedding day in Grandview, December 28, 1881. Looking every bit as dapper as his son would in later years, but self-conscious about his height, Mr. Truman arranged to be seated in this portrait. At five feet four inches, he was two inches shorter than his wife.

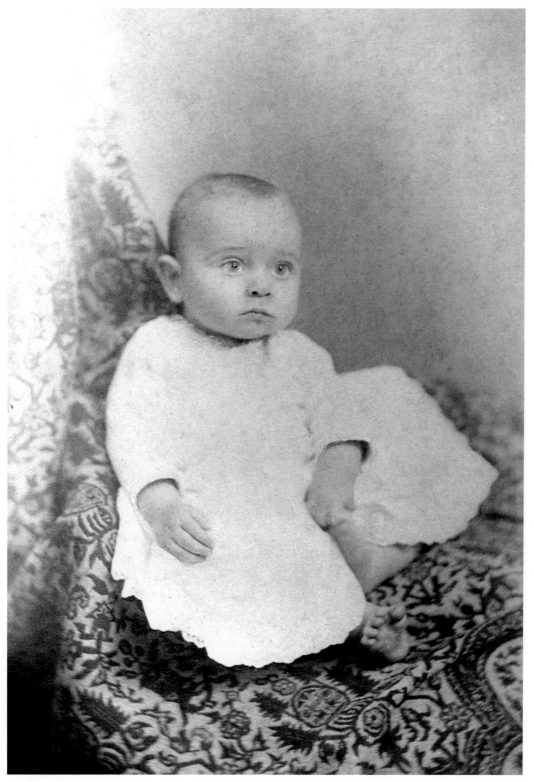

A month-old Harry S. Truman, around 1884. Truman was born in the family farmhouse in Lamar, Missouri, on May 8, 1884. Named for his mother's brother Harrison, his middle name was a problem; it was decided he would share only a middle initial with his grandfathers—Shippe and Solomon.

With an obvious family resemblance, Harry's uncle William Thomas Truman poses for a portrait around 1890. William T. followed cattle interests to Texas, leaving his son Ralph behind with the Missouri Trumans. Harry and Ralph shared a contentious, but brotherly, relationship throughout their lives.

Harriet Louisa Young, around 1890. Always a student of history, Harry gave rapt attention to his maternal grandmother's tales of antebellum life and her family's suffering at the hands of the Union Army— usually told from her rocker on the front porch between puffs on a corncob pipe.

After a run of economic good fortune, John Truman moved his family to this fine home at 909 West Waldo Street in Independence. Here the young Harry flourished amid the social and educational opportunities the town offered. "Our house became headquarters for all the boys and girls around," he later remembered.

Harry at thirteen in 1897. Although no "mama's boy," Harry was under the tutelage of his cultured and well-educated mother and was often teased for his glasses and music lessons. Still, remembered one former playmate, "Sometimes he would surprise the boys and get into a baseball game."

Harry's aunt, Mary Martha Truman, around 1900. Aunt Mattie was educated at Stephens College and served as a teacher in Kansas City. The faraway expression in her eyes may be said to reflect the loneliness she wrote about in letters to friends and family. She died young at the age of 40 in 1900.

Independence High School, Class of 1901. Harry is standing fourth from the left in the back row, while Bess produces a broad grin seated on the far right in the second row. Harry was somewhat rudderless after high school and would knock around several jobs in Kansas City.

Harry visits the family of his father's sister Margaret Noland around 1904. Harry is standing between his cousins Nellie (left) and Ethel (right). They were his constant companions and it was they who provided the spark which rekindled his relationship with Bess—a cake plate which needed returning to the Wallace home.

Mamma Truman at the farmhouse in Grandview. Harry's mother was a college graduate who instilled a love of the arts in her eldest son, but she was no delicate flower. She knew the life of a pioneer wife and was described as lively and spirited. Or, as one family member wrote, "tough as a barrel of roofing nails."

Still lacking direction, Harry enlisted in the National Guard along with some buddies in 1905. Soon after joining, he ventured out to the farm in Grandview to see his grandmother Young. "Harry," he later recounted her saying, "this is the first time since 1863 a blue uniform has been in this house. Don't bring it here again."

During his exile at the farm in Grandview after 1906, Harry visited Independence as often as possible to court Bess. It was not uncommon to see them taking part in a picnic in those days. Here he's accompanied by his future brother-in-law George and George's future wife May Southern along the road leading to the Missouri River.

The Young-Truman farm was the spiritual nexus for several generations of Trumans and associated families. Harry is second from the left in this photo, accompanying his mother, siblings, and cousins at a family event on the farm.

Truman enjoyed the camaraderie he found in Battery B of the Missouri National Guard and was quickly elevated to the rank of corporal. Calling it "the biggest promotion of my life," the affirmation provided him a newfound ambition for leadership.

Harry S. Truman at age 24, around 1908. Although he was no stranger to hard work and long hours operating the J. A. Truman & Son farm at Grandview, Harry always projected a more urbane image more suited to nearby Kansas City. Farmhands later recalled that they never saw Harry in bib overalls.

Harry did not resent the hard work of farming, nor did he enjoy it. He was adept at operating machinery and would later brag about his arrow-straight rows in the fields. Images like this one from around 1910 later helped cultivate Truman's image as a Jeffersonian Democrat and man of the people.

Although the men in this photograph are unidentified, this view may depict one of at least four trips Harry made in conjunction with various land speculation schemes in the Southwest and Northern Plains from 1910 to 1913.

Harry (at the oars) and Bess (with pole) during a fishing trip on the Little Blue River with members of the Wallace clan in August 1913. Sister-in-law May Wallace later recalled that Bess "loved to fish, and Harry didn't . . . so he'd take his book . . . and read and let her fish."

Harry made roundabout trips by train to go from Grandview to Independence. After a cash windfall in 1913, his mother gave him $650 to purchase a used 1911 Stafford touring car, which dramatically increased his mobility—and time spent with Bess on chaperoned dates. Here he rides with Bess, his sister, and cousin Nellie.

Truman was tempted by a number of speculative ventures from 1914 to 1917, including Morgan Oil in 1916. Here he may be standing in front of one of the company's wells in Kansas. Truman and his partners gave up too soon—the company that bought their lease drilled deeper in the same hole and opened up one of the largest oilfields in the Midwest.

Truman (at left, fourth row, beneath the palm trees) was accepted into the Masonic Lodge in the nearby town of Belton, Missouri, in 1909. He enjoyed being a Mason and after forming a new lodge in Grandview, rose to Grand Master for the Grand Lodge of Missouri and ultimately earned the 33rd degree of the Supreme Council of the Scottish Rite.

When America entered World War I, Truman helped organize the expansion of area Guard units into the 129th Field Artillery and was made a lieutenant. This photo was likely taken in 1917, at Fort Sill, Oklahoma, before the unit left for France. Truman is circled at center.

Truman was quickly promoted to captain upon his arrival in France, and his I.D. card shows a rare glimpse of him without eyeglasses. His eyesight was so poor, he constantly worried about losing his glasses and spent his 24-hour leave in New York scaring up three extra pair to take overseas.

Perhaps the most enduring image
of Bess is this angelic pose she
presented to Harry before he left
for France. He carried it with him
throughout his military service, and
it later accompanied him to the
White House.

SERVING

(1919–1944)

Upon returning from the war, Harry S. Truman decided to become a partner in a haberdashery in downtown Kansas City. The store did well initially and became a hangout for veterans, including Truman's friend Jim Pendergast.

Jim's father, Mike, and his uncle, Tom, were powerful players in Jackson County politics, and when they suggested Truman run for office in 1922, Truman took them up on the offer—the store simply wasn't profitable enough to continue. With the help of the Pendergast machine, Truman was easily elected as a county judge, a position similar to a county commissioner in other states.

Truman joined a number of social groups during this period, including the Army Reserve and a Masonic Lodge. He also inquired about membership in the Ku Klux Klan, but rejected them after learning what they were about. This would prove his undoing, though, as they threw their considerable influence against him in his unsuccessful 1924 reelection bid.

The lone bright spot in an otherwise dismal 1924, was the arrival of his daughter, Mary Margaret. Unemployed and with an extra mouth to feed, Truman took a job selling auto club memberships. But he had had a taste of politics and he liked it. In 1926, and again in 1930, he ran successfully for presiding judge. During his eight years in that position, he built a reputation for honesty and integrity in office. He refused to be tainted by his association with the Pendergasts and felt that his actions were his vindication.

This paid a dividend in 1934 when Pendergast, put on the defensive by reformers, decided to support clean-living Truman for U.S. Senator. Though not much of a speaker, Truman could communicate well with the common man. He survived a fierce battle for the Democratic nomination and then easily defeated his Republican opponent. He would face another tough election battle in 1940, this time alone, after Tom Pendergast had gone to prison on bribery charges. He won by the narrowest of margins.

In the Senate, he maintained his tough, honest approach to government, supported the New Deal, and quickly made powerful friends in Washington, including Vice-president John Nance Garner. He also became known as a keen-eyed investigator on the Interstate Commerce Committee and the committee examining waste and graft in defense contracts, known as the Truman Committee. His career did not go unnoticed by President Franklin D. Roosevelt.

In March 1919, Harry (fourth from left, second row) and fellow officers of the 129th Field Artillery were billeted in the Chateau le Chenay near Courcemont, France. They would sail for home within a month.

Harry and Bess married at Trinity Episcopal Church in Independence on June 28, 1919. Each in their mid-thirties, they were considered late bloomers by the standards of the day. Indeed, daughter Margaret later said if the war had not come along they might have waited until they were fifty, "and I might never have gotten here."

Whether an act of economic desperation or an attempt to impress his future mother-in-law, Harry impulsively entered into a partnership with Army buddy Eddie Jacobson to operate this haberdashery at 104 West 12th, Kansas City. The location was ideal and sales were good—for a while.

Until a general recession forced it to close, Truman & Jacobson was a popular hangout for veterans of the 129th Field Artillery. One frequent visitor was Jim Pendergast, who brought in his politician father Mike to meet the well-respected former captain—Harry Truman.

Kansas City's Muehlebach Hotel was the setting for the third annual St. Patrick's Day reunion banquet of Battery D. Truman (#1, seated, left-center) would maintain close ties with the men of his unit throughout his life.

Always active in civic organizations, Harry (standing at left-center) is photographed in Kansas City's Swope Park on an outing of the Triangle Club, a merchant's group similar to the Rotary Club, in 1921.

Harry earned a reputation as a can-do guy when he helped organize the Armistice Day parade and dedication of the Liberty Memorial in Kansas City in November 1921. Here he stands (facing the camera, in uniform, behind the man in the suit) in review of the 129th Field Artillery as they present the flags of each of the Allies.

Truman is seen here (seated, at center) as presiding judge for Jackson County, around 1927. Despite his association with Kansas City's Pendergast machine, Truman quickly earned a reputation for honesty and effectiveness. Voters returned him in 1931 by an overwhelming majority.

Truman built a number of strong friendships while he remained active in the Army Reserves throughout the interwar period. Here he is seen with John Snyder (center), who would become Truman's Secretary of the Treasury, and Harry Vaughan (to Snyder's left), one of his most trusted military aides.

Truman poses next to a Studebaker, around 1930. It was not uncommon for Truman to take research trips by automobile. Before building Jackson County's two new courthouses, he drove more than 24,000 miles at his own expense examining other buildings around the country.

Truman is sworn in for a second term as presiding judge for Jackson County, in 1931. With a mandate from the people, Truman worked tirelessly on public projects in the face of a worsening Depression. His penchant for good government helped deflect constant criticism that he was simply an operative of the Pendergast machine.

Truman (second from right) with county officials at the dedication of the new highway system, in 1932. Truman's modernization of Jackson County's roads during this term is now legendary. The new roads were no longer shoddily built "pie crusts," and no farm was more than two miles from a main road.

Truman on horseback in the Ozarks, around 1933. One of Harry's longtime friends recalled, "When he was up here in the courthouse things would get tough, you know, get worrisome; he'd get three or four [guys] and get in the car and go down to the Ozarks and stay three or four days."

Truman's "sound car" for his first Senate campaign, October 1934. Only months before, Truman was involved in an Olympian struggle for control of Missouri's Democratic Party by St. Louis and Kansas City factions. He and the Pendergast machine won the nomination by a slender margin.

Truman's campaign "sound car" plies the streets of Poplar Bluff. Largely unknown outside Jackson County, Truman barnstormed the state during the fall campaign against Republican Roscoe Patterson. Many believed Truman's victory was a cinch, but he campaigned tirelessly nonetheless.

Harry speaks from a farm truck in Sikeston, Missouri, October 1934. A politician from the state's "bootheel" later recalled that "Truman was unusually popular in southeast Missouri." The *Kansas City Times* reported that Truman won the primary "in the creek forks and grass roots," continuing to remind voters that "I am for the individual, the common run of mankind."

The candidate relaxes with campaign workers on the campaign trail in Greenville, Missouri, October 1934. Harry sailed to victory by some 250,000 votes.

Truman as seen aboard the Naval Reserve gunboat USS *Dubuque*, around 1935. This photograph was probably taken during joint summer exercises between the Army and Navy reserves on the Great Lakes.

Truman (center) listens in on John Nance Garner of Texas, around 1936. Garner, Franklin D. Roosevelt's first vice-president, made fast friends with Truman and showed the junior senator from Missouri the ropes in Washington.

Truman (left) and Tom Pendergast (to Truman's left) at the 1936 Democratic Convention in Philadelphia. During his first term, critics referred to Truman as "the Senator from Pendergast." For his part, Pendergast advised Truman, "Work hard, keep your mouth shut, and answer your mail."

A deer-hunting party near St. Mary's, Pennsylvania, in 1937. Truman is on the far left, a guest of his friend Senator Joseph Guffey of Pennsylvania. Despite Truman's 53 years, he and Guffey were considered "young Turks" in the Senate.

Senator Truman inspects Fort Knox, in January 1938. His guide is General Daniel van Voorhis, dubbed "Grandfather of the Armored Force" for his early mechanization of former cavalry units at Fort Knox.

Ever popular on "the Hill," Truman (second from right) secured an invitation to the exclusive Alfalfa Club's annual summer event. Guests were required to wear masks and pledge to "put aside all cares today, State and personal, and to be a boy again."

Senator Truman observes the artillery firing range on an inspection tour of his former post at Fort Sill, Oklahoma, in November 1939.

In November 1939, Truman took part in an inspection tour of a dozen defense installations by armed forces committees of both houses. Trips like this one were instrumental in preparing the senator to lead the famous Truman Committee investigations of the military.

Senator Truman, a man
of increasing importance,
descends the steps of the
U.S. Capitol in 1940.

Sedalia was the state headquarters for Truman's reelection bid in 1940. With Tom Pendergast in prison, Truman was forced to rely on his own political clout and the help of the support network he'd built in Missouri over the preceding twenty years.

Truman (lower right) appears at a campaign rally in Washington in 1940. Despite being in the political fight of his life back home, he carried a full workload at the Capitol because of a world in crisis.

Campaign workers assemble in front of the headquarters in Sedalia in 1940. Money was scarce and the rhetoric fierce, but Truman found ways to deliver his message—and FDR's—to the people of Missouri. He won by a hairbreadth—8,000 votes.

Senator Truman receives a Christmas gift from an official of the American Trucking Association. Truman worked to reform national transportation policy into a uniform code. Although the Wheeler-Truman Act of 1940 did not make everyone happy, most agreed it was fair.

One of the successes of the Truman Committee was Ford's Willow Run Plant in Detroit. After the Committee's investigation, the "Willit Run? Plant" was transformed into one of the nation's most efficient. Always happy to tickle the ivories, Truman found time to entertain Senator Homer Ferguson of Michigan during the investigation.

Senator Truman was a tireless watchdog of the people's purse and frequently made inspection tours of government facilities.

Truman and members of the Truman Committee dine at the Peabody Hotel in Memphis, around 1941, probably during an inspection of an inefficient ordnance plant near Milan, Tennessee.

Truman always felt in good company with fellow veterans. Here he addresses the local American Legion at the Pocahontas Theatre in Welsh, West Virginia.

Senator Truman, accompanied by Undersecretary of War Robert Patterson, is back home in Missouri during an inspection of Fort Leonard Wood, August 21, 1942.

Truman listens intently during a session of the Truman Committee, around 1942. The committee won wide acclaim for Truman and he was proud of his efforts in such important work. "We saved the taxpayers about fifteen billion dollars," he would later boast.

Senator Harry and members of the Truman Committee meet in Kansas City in early December 1942 to
investigate inefficiencies in the fuel oil and gasoline distribution system after rationing was enforced. "It seems
to me we could use a little horse sense," Truman told the federal official in charge.

Truman takes time out for a photo opportunity with a quartet of War Bond Concert winners, around 1943.

Senator Truman inspects the North American Aviation bomber plant in Kansas City, Kansas, around 1943. This highly efficient plant produced more than 6,000 of the Army's 10,000 B-25 Mitchell bombers.

Mightily swinging a magnum of champagne made from Missouri grapes, George Washington University sophomore Margaret Truman christens the massive battleship *Missouri,* giving it a good kick in the bow when it refused to slide from its moorings. It took a full minute for the ship to slip into the water.

Senator Truman with the Missouri delegation at the 1944 Democratic National Convention in Chicago. Truman made it known to all who would listen that he did not want the job of vice-president. As he told daughter Margaret, the White House "is a nice address, but I wouldn't want to move in through the back door."

Mamma Truman, proud as ever of her Harry, during the 1944 campaign. An active campaigner despite her 91 years, she organized women voters in Grandview and carried out a telephone campaign to rally the vote. "I knew Harry would be all right after I heard him give that fine speech in Congress," she said.

Truman on an inspection tour of Camp Crowder near Neosho, Missouri, August 30, 1944. Having resigned his chairmanship of the Truman Committee on August 3, he nonetheless remained involved in defense matters.

Inspecting a mock jungle at Camp Crowder. The next day Truman would kick off his campaign for the vice-presidency at his birthplace in nearby Lamar. Tens of thousands arrived to support the "Show Me" state's new favorite son and overwhelmed the little town.

The Trumans arrive in Pittsburgh, Pennsylvania, on November 2, 1944. Pittsburgh was the last stop of a grueling 8,000-mile transcontinental campaign tour. Bess did not enjoy their new life; early in the campaign she is said to have glared at Harry and remarked, "Are we going to have to go through this for the rest of our lives?"

Upon recovering from the revelry of election night, Truman boarded a plane for the flight from Missouri back to Washington, November 9, 1944. Here he reads the newspaper in perhaps the last solitude he would have for some time.

The *Washington Post* estimated 330,000 people thronged the route from Union Station to the White House to welcome back "the Champ" (FDR) from his home in New York, November 10, 1944. Here he expresses his gratitude to the nation for returning him to Washington as Harry waits patiently beside him.

LEADING

(1945–1952)

In 1944, President Franklin D. Roosevelt sought a running mate who would appeal to the center of a fraying Democratic Party. He did not seek or want the job, but Senator Harry S. Truman was selected by FDR, and, in the same way he had responded to his father's requests, Truman agreed out of a sense of duty.

He would serve only 82 days. When FDR died in April 1945, Truman stepped unflinchingly into the role of President. The war in Europe was all but won, and there was great tension in the capital regarding the invasion of Japan.

In the first four months of his inherited term, he oversaw creation of the United Nations, faced off with Joseph Stalin at Potsdam over the postwar landscape of Europe, and made the fateful decision to use the atomic bomb to end the war with Japan.

The 1946 election year was troublesome for him as he struggled with ways to manage the postwar economy and find a middle ground between inflation and recession. Many of his solutions, including his handling of significant labor strikes and price controls, were not popular among voters, leading to Republican control of Congress.

Alongside troubles at home, postwar Europe remained volatile in the face of Soviet aggression. In response, Truman boldly stated American policy in early 1947 in what became known as the Truman Doctrine: the United States would intervene anytime and anywhere to defend the principles of democracy. Essentially, this was the declaration of the Cold War. The most notable outgrowths of this policy were the Marshall Plan for the economic recovery of Europe and the Berlin Airlift.

Truman, never cautious, made controversial advances in civil rights in 1948 despite its being an election year; most notably, he integrated the armed forces. His reelection bid for 1948 was one of the most memorable in the annals of national elections. Discounted by the media and battling a split in the Democratic Party, he took his fight to the people in an exhausting whistle-stop tour by train and won a dramatic come-from-behind victory.

Foreign affairs in his second term were dominated by the first crucial test of the Truman Doctrine—the Korean War—and U.S. entry into the NATO alliance. At home, Truman faced an unruly Congress: his Fair Deal, a set of sweeping social reforms, was quashed, and Senator Joseph McCarthy conducted a misguided hunt for communists. He also renovated the dilapidated White House, taking up residence in Blair House across the street, where in 1950 an attempt was made on his life by Puerto Rican nationalists.

Margaret, Harry, and Bess arrive at the White House for Franklin D. Roosevelt's fourth inauguration, January 20, 1945. Ice and sleet pelted the small crowd assembled on the south portico. Owing perhaps to his poor health, FDR delivered one of the shortest inaugural addresses in history.

Vice-president Truman was the guest of honor at the USO's fourth anniversary celebration in February 1945. Bess (at center, on the sailor's right) dutifully maintained her busy calendar as Second Lady despite complaining that her handshaking arm was still swollen from receiving 4,000 guests on inauguration day.

Hollywood star Lana Turner arrived in Washington during the first week of March 1945 to promote her latest film *Keep Your Powder Dry* and make appearances for the USO and Red Cross. Here she has taken Vice-president Truman and Admiral William Halsey by the arm.

Vice-president Truman is introduced to an unidentified man by Chicago mayor Edward Kelly during a St. Patrick's Day event at the Stevens Hotel in Chicago, March 1945. In his speech, Truman gave Americans a glimpse of his presidency when he said, "No nation on this globe should be more internationally minded than America."

Just days before the presidency is thrust upon him, Truman tours Virginia's Fort Belvoir with commanding Brigadier General Gordon R. Young (at center) and longtime friend and aide Harry H. Vaughan (right), April 4, 1945.

President Truman's official portrait, 1945. Upon hearing the news of Franklin's death from Eleanor Roosevelt, Truman said, "Is there anything I can do for you?" Shaking her head she replied, "Is there anything we can do for you? For you are the one in trouble now."

President Truman receives a gift from his old political ally Bryce Smith, former mayor of Kansas City, around 1945.

At 9:00 A.M. on May 8, 1945, President Truman addressed the nation from his desk via radio to announce the unconditional surrender of German forces. He asked the nation not to forget the "terrible price we have paid to rid the world of Hitler and his evil band" but reminded them that "our victory is but half won."

The president grins for the camera as he cuts the cake in celebration of his 61st birthday, May 8, 1945. It was truly a happy occasion; in addition to the news of victory in Europe, it was also the family's first day as residents of the White House.

The *Sacred Cow* (the official airplane) brought Mamma Truman to Washington on May 11, 1945. At 92 she explored the White House on her own and was overheard at dinner asking whether a certain person was a Yankee. When her son told her it was true, she said, "Well, if there are any good Yankees, I haven't seen one yet."

Eleanor Roosevelt joins President Truman as he presents a posthumous Distinguished Service Medal to the widow of Major General Edwin M. Watson, June 8, 1945. Watson was FDR's most trusted military aide and served him for nearly the entirety of his four terms in office.

T. V. Soong, Chinese Foreign Minister (center), visits President Truman and acting Secretary of State Joseph C. Grew in Washington on his way to the United Nations conference in San Francisco, June 9, 1945. China was a powerful ally, having helped finance the "Flying Tigers," volunteer pilots who joined the fray against Japan before the United States entered the war.

The Association of Radio News Analysts poses with President Truman in the White House, June 16, 1945. The group was a collection of about 20 radio pundits who lobbied for more freedom of information during wartime.

In what would today be informally called a clash of "alpha males," Truman and Eisenhower never really liked each other. Here the two meet at National Airport early on the morning of June 19, 1945—Truman was headed to the West Coast and Ike to a hero's ticker-tape parade in New York City.

Truman rides with Washington governor Mon C. Wallgren on June 19, 1945. Before attending the United Nations conference in San Francisco, President Truman made a 13-hour flight from Washington, D.C., to Olympia, Washington—the first president to fly within the U.S. while in office.

Governor Wallgren was a favorite of the President's when the two served on the Truman Committee in the Senate. Although the trip was a holiday for Truman, he made a surprise appearance at a concert in the capitol rotunda and briefly spoke to the 3,000 people in attendance.

Truman donned a Cowichan sweater
and bowtie for a salmon fishing junket
on the Puget Sound, June 21, 1945.

Now in more traditional garb, the President with Governor Wallgren tells reporters fish stories. Truman's old friend Harry Vaughan is in uniform behind him. The president didn't hook any salmon, but did manage to reel in a dogfish.

Huge crowds line the steps of a building in Portland, Oregon, as the president makes a two-hour stopover on his way to San Francisco. Later in the day, he would speak at the veterans' hospital on Marquam Hill and announce that General Omar Bradley would oversee veterans' affairs. "Nothing is too good for them," he said.

Truman is greeted at the Portland Army Air Base by a military band, high-ranking Democrats, and base personnel on June 26, 1945. While reviewing a line of WACs, Truman turned to one with a bright smile and asked her where she hailed from. "Kansas!" she replied. He was visibly pleased to meet someone he considered a neighbor.

A 21-gun salute and a military rendition of the "Missouri Waltz" greeted Truman as he arrived at Hamilton Field in San Francisco on June 26, 1945. A crowd of staggering proportions, estimated at 500,000 by officials, cheered as he paraded throughout the city. "It's the office and what it stands for they're cheering—not me," he said.

At the conclusion of the nine-week United Nations Conference on International Organization on June 26, 1945, Truman addressed the delegates of the fifty nations assembled in San Francisco. "You have created a great instrument for peace," he told them. "The world must now use it!"

Margaret greets her father in Kansas City on June 27, 1945. She was sent home to Missouri for the summer after her father discovered that her active social life was a regular feature of capital newspapers. *Washington Post* columnist Drew Pearson came to her defense in print, saying her behavior was "only natural exuberance on the part of a college girl who found herself First Daughter of the Land."

The president is flanked by his brother and daughter as they leave Fairfax Airport in Kansas City. The Secret Service initially planned to have Truman slip into town quietly, but he overruled them and ordered an open car to take him through downtown Kansas City and home to Independence.

Thousands of Jackson County faithful welcome Truman home. "All these people have seen me two or three times a day, for the last 30 or 40 years. I can't see what there is about me now that would make them turn out like they did today," he quipped.

Truman makes a final wave to the crowds before retiring inside the family home on Delaware Street as a Secret Service man holds the door. His old neighborhood was transformed into a security zone as two dozen agents milled around his yard and white-helmeted MPs patrolled the streets.

Truman and his naval aide James K. Vardaman in June 1945. Vardaman, an old friend from St. Louis, accompanied Truman to the United Nations conference in San Francisco and for a few days during a layover in Independence.

Ever the man of the people, President Truman shares mess with sailors aboard the USS *Augusta* en route to the Potsdam Conference in July 1945.

Thousands of cheering Belgians lined the River Scheldt in Antwerp to welcome the American president to Europe. Secretary of State James Byrnes and Truman's friend and aide Harry Vaughan (standing) are aboard the USS *Augusta*, July 15, 1945.

The *Augusta* was escorted across the English Channel into the Scheldt Estuary by an American cruiser and three British destroyers. Here, Truman and Byrnes return the salute given by the assembled crew lining the deck of the HMS *Hambledon*.

Greeting the president as he debarked was a delegation of Belgian officials. Here he is received by the Burgomeister of Antwerp, Camille Huysmans.

The "Little White House" in the Berlin suburb of Babelsburg, July 13, 1945. Attending the Potsdam Conference, Truman was told it belonged to a German movie executive. Eleven years later, he received a letter from one of the family relating the horrors suffered at the hands of Russian soldiers. They were living in squalor 500 yards away during the conference.

One of the rooms in the three-story residence of the American delegation. In his diary, Truman described it as "a dirty yellow and red . . . comfortable enough all around, but what a nightmare it would give an interior decorator."

On the morning of July 16, 1945, the British delegation called on the president. Among those making the two-block trip to the "Little White House" were Prime Minister Winston Churchill (lower left) and his daughter Junior Commander Mary Churchill (shaking hands with Truman).

After Joseph Stalin delayed the opening of the Potsdam Conference, Truman surprised the Secret Service by ordering an impromptu tour of Berlin. He was awed by the destruction in the German capital and upon seeing these ruins of the Reichschancellery remarked, "It's just a demonstration of what happens when a man overreaches himself."

On the afternoon of July 18, 1945, Truman and three of his closest aides walked the two blocks to Churchill's residence to return the visit paid them earlier. Here the president greets Captain Francis of the 2nd Battalion, Scots.

On July 20, 1945, Truman stands at attention with generals Eisenhower (left) and Patton (center) as the Flag of Liberation is raised over the American zone in Berlin. His impromptu address was short, but timeless: "We want to see the time come when we can do the things in peace that we have been able to do in war."

Because he was the only official head of state, President Truman was selected as chairman by the other two members of the Big Three. Proceedings moved slowly and the third session (pictured here) convened for only 50 minutes, July 19, 1945.

The Big Three perform a triple handshake at Potsdam, July 23, 1945. Sizing up the two in his diary, Truman said, "I can get along with Stalin. He is honest—but smart as hell." And of Churchill, "We can get along fine if he doesn't try to give me too much soft soap."

Major General Floyd Parks presents the Flag of Liberation, which was flying over the U.S. Capitol the day Pearl Harbor was attacked. It was flown above each conquered capital. Tokyo would be next.

This iconic image of the Big Three was taken in the gardens at Cecilienhof in Potsdam. Initially, Truman felt, and newspapers opined, that he was the intellectual lesser at the conference table. He became more confident, though, writing in his diary, "I told 'em [the] U.S. had ceased to give away its assets without returns."

Truman received England's King George VI aboard the *Augusta* at Plymouth, August 2, 1945. Truman later wrote in his diary that the king impressed him as a good man. However, an aide later recalled that the president had poked him in the ribs and said, "You don't get to see kings every day, especially if you're a farm boy from Missouri."

On August 14, 1945, the president, backed by his cabinet, assembled more than 200 members of the media in his office and beamed as he read the news of the unconditional surrender of Japan following the dropping of two atomic bombs. He would later say, "I don't believe in speculating on mental feeling and as far as the bomb was concerned I ordered its use for a military reason . . . and it saved the lives of a great many of our soldiers."

At a ceremony on the White House lawn, President Truman pins the Congressional Medal of Honor on Marine PFC Franklin Sigler, October 5, 1945. In his remarks, Truman said, "I would rather have that medal, the Congressional Medal of Honor, than to be President of the United States."

In a joint session of Congress on October 23, 1945, the president outlined a plan for universal military training. In lieu of a draft, boys 18 to 20 would be required to spend a year of their lives in military training, thereby creating a large reserve force. The nation having had enough of war, the plan was widely panned.

For Navy Day, October 27, 1945, the president was given a reception only New York City could give—more than 5,000,000 citizens lined his seven-mile parade route. Here he is signing a document aboard the USS *Missouri*.

At Westminster College in Fulton, Missouri, Truman and Winston Churchill receive honorary degrees, March 5, 1946. In Churchill's lecture he called on the U.S. to defend Europe against Soviet aggression. His words would add to the lexicon of the cold war: "An iron curtain has descended across the continent."

On Army Day, April 6, 1946, Truman addresses a crowd at Chicago's Soldier Field. This speech, in which he said America would remain strong in order to protect the weak, represented his growing confidence in foreign affairs. The *London Times* declared it to be his "most statesmanlike speech" since becoming president.

A moment of solitude on the White House lawn, spring 1946. It was cherry blossom time, but also time for the star magnolia, pictured here.

President Truman grins as he receives a report from motion picture industry executives.
The group received praise for the success of their annual Red Cross fund drive.

When stormy seas cast a pall over the president's vacation in New England aboard the official yacht *Williamsburg,* he ordered a turn south to Bermuda. Arriving on August 22, 1946, Truman became the first American president to visit Bermuda while in office. Here he tours the island in the governor's ceremonial landau.

Field Marshal Bernard Montgomery pays a brief courtesy call on President Truman at the White House during a tour of West Point and other American military facilities on the East Coast, September 11, 1946.

Harry and Margaret return home to Independence to vote in the 1946 congressional election. In one of the biggest political mistakes of his career, Truman chose to bow out of campaigning for fellow Democrats. Republicans took control of both houses of Congress in a landslide.

In November 1946, the president retired to Key West, Florida, for a week of much needed rest. During the trip he submerged 450 feet in a captured German U-boat to become the first president to travel underwater in a submarine. He also picked up the knack for deep-sea fishing, as seen here.

Perfect weather greeted the president in Florida during his vacation at the Key West Naval Station. Here he and naval aide Captain James Foskett leave the base commandant's house for a morning swim. Truman and subsequent presidents would return here so often, the house would become known as the Little White House.

In his White House office on January 16, 1947, President Truman makes peace with the "big six"—leaders of both parties in the new Republican-controlled Congress. Truman professed a desire for non-partisanship and cooperation, and all agreed the meeting ended in a spirit of goodwill.

Winter descends on the Truman family home on Delaware Street in Independence, around 1947. Soon after this photograph was made, iron fencing was erected around the home to stop the ravages of souvenir seekers.

Braving ice and snow, President Truman travels to Mount Vernon to lay a commemorative wreath on the grave of George Washington, February 22, 1947.

A defiant President Truman, addressing a joint session of Congress on March 12, 1947, declares that America will not stand idly by while the free world is crushed under the boot of communism. Of this new Truman Doctrine, *Newsweek* said, "If words could shape the future of nations, these unquestionably would."

In March 1947, ostensibly to recuperate from the stresses of recent weeks, the president retired once again to Key West with several of his military advisors. Undoubtedly strategies for waging the new "Cold War" were foremost in their discussions. Here they bask in the Florida sun on the lawn of the Little White House.

Before returning to Washington, President Truman was presented with a cup from Virginia Kelly, Queen of the Key West International Fishing Tournament. The president's party competed in a special White House Sweepstakes division of the tournament. Naturally, the president won the cup for Best Fish—a 4-pound mackerel.

Truman greets opposing managers Ossie Bluege of the Senators (center) and the Yankees' Bucky Harris at the opening of the Washington baseball season. When tossing out the opening pitch, the president amused the crowd. After being announced as a southpaw, he threw first right-handed and then with his natural left hand.

More than 600,000 Washingtonians lined the five-mile route from National Airport to the White House to welcome Mexican president Miguel Aleman. Observers believed it was the largest—and warmest—welcome ever given a foreign visitor in the city's history.

Moments before Truman (at center) ascended the reviewing stand at the 35th Infantry Division Reunion in Kansas City, June 7, 1947, he leapt from his moving car behind the Honor Guard and marched alongside them. He'd been there before—the troops in front were the men of his old command, Battery D of the 129th Field Artillery.

Once, present, and future presidents are photographed together on June 17, 1947, at the bicentennial of Princeton University. All three, Eisenhower (left), Truman (center), and Hoover (right), received honorary degrees. This was Truman's tenth honorary degree—but he was the last president never to have attended college.

The Little White House was once again the president's vacation choice in December of 1947. Here he shoots some footage with his movie camera around the Key West Naval Station. One official duty during the trip was to dedicate the country's newest national park—Florida's Everglades.

Truman and Army Secretary Kenneth Royall observe the transfer of power from Chief of Staff Eisenhower
(left) to General Omar N. Bradley. Eisenhower supported Truman's policies, but resented his relationship with
General George Marshall and resigned to become president of Columbia University, February 7, 1948.

As free Europe faced Soviet aggression, the president battled a balky Republican Congress. Before a joint session on March 17, 1948, he again called for bold American action in defense of freedom. "There is some risk involved in action—there always is," he said. "But there is far more risk in failure to act."

Over the Memorial Day holiday, 1948, the president sailed in the yacht *Williamsburg* to Annapolis, Maryland, to tour the Naval Academy. Here (in white hat) he leaves the docks en route to watching crew races and an Army-Navy baseball game.

The president made a brief stop on his Memorial weekend cruise to place a wreath at the Tomb of the Unknown Soldier in Arlington National Cemetery. "This country is made up of all races and all creeds . . . and we live peaceably side-by-side," he said. "That is our ambition for the whole world."

Perhaps backing up some of his tough talk on the campaign trail, President Truman takes aim with a shotgun during a brief layover at the Sun Valley resort in Idaho, June 7, 1948. He was on a whistle-stop tour of the western states.

The apolitical dedication of New York's new Idlewild International Airport was the setting for this historic meeting between Governor Thomas Dewey of New York and President Truman, July 31, 1948. Never before had two opposing major party candidates for president shared the same stage during a campaign.

After the revolt by Southern Democrats during the 1948 reelection campaign, one response was the formation of Truman-Barkley clubs to generate grassroots funds and support. Here members of the Missouri club meet in St. Louis behind photos of the candidates in summer of that year.

As Truman bid adieu to clamorous crowds in St. Louis after his Cinderella election-night victory, a man thrust the *Chicago Tribune* into his hands—the headline read "DEWEY DEFEATS TRUMAN." Photographers captured the historic gaffe held high by a jubilant Truman. "That's one for the book!" he quipped to riotous cheers.

Even Washington officials underestimated the President upon his return to the city on November 5, 1948. They had prepared for a crowd of 500,000, but nearly 750,000 turned out to welcome him home. The *Washington Post* said, "It was a warm and happy salute to a gallant fighter who had everything against him—but the people."

This is the last portrait of President Truman with his cabinet before his second inauguration, January 14, 1949. No big changes were afoot except for the upcoming arrival of the formidable Secretary of State, Dean Acheson. Vice-president Barkley is seated on Truman's left.

After taking the oath of office on January 20, 1949, the president gave a matter-of-fact, but powerful, speech. Concerned that their applause, hands gloved against the cold, was too muffled, the 40,000 people in attendance made thunderous rumbles on the wooden bleachers with their feet.

Best estimates were that 1,000,000 people lined Pennsylvania Avenue as the president and vice-president paraded to the White House on inauguration day. On direct orders from President Truman, it was the first time in history black Americans were admitted to all inaugural functions.

One of the Trumans' best friends in Washington was Oklahoma heiress Perle Mesta (left), seen here with Bess (at far-left), Harry, and Margaret (third from right) at the inaugural ball on January 20, 1949. Though famous for her parties, she was a powerful woman in her own right and Truman soon named her Ambassador to Luxembourg.

For most of his presidency, Truman met weekly with the Democratic Party leadership—the Big Four. Pictured here are (left to right) Speaker of the House Sam Rayburn, the President, the Vice-president, Senate Majority Leader Ernest McFarland, and House Majority Leader John McCormack.

In October 1951, Assistant Secretary of Defense Anna Rosenberg initiated a drive to recruit more women into the military. Truman trusted Rosenberg, a brilliant planner and organizer, to provide him with the manpower—or personnel—to pursue his war of containment against the Soviet Communists.

When Britain's young Princess Elizabeth visited in November 1951, Truman's daughter Margaret warned him that everyone who meets the princess falls in love with her. He may not have, but at the state dinner in her honor he wistfully began his toast, "When I was a little boy, there was a fairy princess." Gesturing her way he added, "And there she is."

After a piano nearly fell through the ceiling in 1948, newly reelected President Truman asked Congress to authorize a $5.7 million renovation of the White House. During the three-year job, the family lived across the street in Blair House. Here Harry and Bess return to their recently redone digs, March 27, 1952.

Queen Juliana of the Netherlands arrived in Washington on April 2, 1952. Juliana was a modern monarch who largely dispensed with formality and interacted with common people. She found one in President Truman. With a beaming smile he greeted her with his customary informality, "I hope you have a grand time here!"

Truman with Arkansas officials at the dedication of the massive Bull Shoals Dam, July 2, 1952. Truman told voters a Republican would reverse the progress of the New Deal. "We can't turn the clock back," he said. "It just won't run that way . . . we have to keep on fighting the pullbacks . . . the standpatters . . . and the reactionaries."

The Trumans gather at the entrance to the White House on Christmas Eve, 1952. After asking the nation to pray for world peace and the well-being of the fighting men in Korea, the president lit the National Christmas Tree for the last time.

REFLECTING

(1953–1972)

President Harry S. Truman was ambivalent about running for reelection in 1952. The Republican Congress had amended the Constitution to allow a president to serve no more than two terms, but he received an exemption if he chose to run in 1952. He did not campaign and after a poor showing in the New Hampshire primary, he made the decision not to run. His grudging admiration for Dwight D. Eisenhower turned sour later that year as the latter ran for the Republicans with a platform based on criticism of the Truman administration.

In 1953, Truman found himself a private citizen in much the same position he had faced thirty years before when the haberdashery closed: unemployed with no savings. At the time executive branch employees were not awarded pensions, so Truman received no compensation for his government service (until 1958), except his monthly veteran's stipend.

Returning to Independence, and buoyed by a personal loan, he undertook the writing of his Memoirs and the planning and fundraising for his presidential library. The Memoirs were completed in 1955, but despite their critical and commercial success, they did not secure his financial future. Harry and his siblings sold the family farm in Grandview that year and realized enough profit to live out his days in relative comfort. The Truman Library was built in 1957 about half a mile from the Truman home in Independence. The project was paid for entirely with private funds and then transferred to the public.

Truman was often dismayed at what he perceived as disrespect by succeeding presidents, most of whom did not seek his advice or afford him a leadership role in the party. A courtesy visit during a stopover in Kansas City was often his only contact with these men. Still, the press did not ignore him and he never failed to launch one of his missiles of truth at candidates in either party if he were asked. One of the happiest moments of his post-presidential life was President Lyndon Johnson's signing of the Medicare bill at the Truman Library in 1965—it had been a component of Truman's Fair Deal.

Harry's health went into steady decline after this time; he had suffered a fall and no longer took his mile-long walks around town. In his final days he made arrangements for his funeral and final resting place. On December 26, 1972, he passed away at the age of 88. Bess would remain in the house on Delaware Street until she joined Harry in 1982 at the age of 97.

A private citizen now, Truman was made an "honorary chieftain" by the Oklahoma Junior Chamber of Commerce (Jay Cees) at a ceremony in Kansas City on June 7, 1953. He held his warbonnet high but refused to put it on because, "I don't want to look like Calvin Coolidge."

In Milwaukee to address the annual convention of the American Federation of Musicians, Truman played a duet of "Hail, Hail, the Gang's All Here" with Federation president James Petrillo, on June 15, 1954. The piano would follow him back to the Truman Library as a gift from the Federation.

Between 1953 and 1957, Truman was actively involved in fundraising for the Truman Library. In this photo he shares a press conference with philanthropist Cyrus S. Eaton at Eaton's home in Northfield, Ohio, June 3, 1955.

After World War II, General Eisenhower gave President Truman a beautiful globe from his office in Europe. It was Truman's favorite fixture in the Oval Office, but he returned it to Eisenhower at the transfer of power. Here, in 1955, Truman examines a copy, which is now on exhibit in the Oval Office replica at the Truman Library.

Unlike most of his predecessors, Truman had no previous career, family fortune, or business interests to fall back on when he left office. He relied on personal loans to pay the bills until he received payment for his completed Memoirs in 1955. Here he signs a copy for Barbara Bosley at his office in Kansas City.

Margaret married Clifton Daniel in Independence on April 21, 1956. The engagement was a surprise to her parents. Truman got this advice from friend Dean Acheson: "All and all the father of the bride is a pitiable creature. No one bothers with him at all. His only comforter is a bottle of good bourbon. Have you plenty on hand?"

Harry and his siblings sold the family farm in Grandview to shopping-center developers on August 23, 1955. Harry's brother Vivian (left) is seen here with Harry and two other men at the farm. The three siblings made enough from the proceeds to live comfortably for the rest of their lives.

On his 72nd birthday, May 8, 1956, Harry and Bess embark on a two-month trip to Europe. Before departing from the Independence train station, he was feted by newsmen and photographers, who presented him with a birthday cake. Here he shares the wealth with some of the younger travelers at the station.

Appalled by news of mistreated black veterans, President Truman had created a committee to oversee the integration of the military. One member of that group was John Sengstacke, editor of the *Chicago Defender,* seen here riding in the city's annual Bud Billiken Day Parade between Truman and Mayor Richard J. Daley, in August 1956.

Officers of the French cruise line Compagnie Générale Transatlantique meet with Truman around 1957. The occasion for this photo was undocumented, though it may have been in connection with his continued fundraising efforts for the Truman Library.

Chief Justice Earl Warren (left) joins Truman (at center) and other Masons in the
Masonic ceremony for laying the cornerstone at the Truman Library, July 6, 1957.

Former President Herbert Hoover (seated at left, wearing fedora) looks on as Archivist of the United States Wayne Grover (center) accepts the transfer of the Truman Library to "the people" during the dedication on July 6, 1957.

Truman receives an honorary American Farmer degree from John Haid, President of the Future Farmers of America, during the group's annual convention in Kansas City, October 15, 1957. "You boys have the best chance of anyone in the nation to keep this country great," he encouraged them.

Former President Truman poses with Donald McSween (second from left) and two others in his office at the Truman Library, around 1958. McSween held many executive offices in Tennessee and had become a friend of Truman in his later years. Truman enjoyed visiting McSween's East Tennessee home and being "among my kind of people."

Truman greets security guard William Story at the Truman Library on his 74th birthday, May 8, 1958. His doctors admonished him to curtail his activities, but "I can still outwalk any of them," he said. He would enjoy a luncheon with 70 well-wishers that same afternoon.

Truman arrives in St. Louis for the 1958 conference of the Missouri chapter of the American Legion. Although he and President Eisenhower carried out a smoldering feud, Truman told the assembled Show-Me State veterans to support Eisenhower during the crisis in Lebanon and the Middle East.

Jackson McBride of Honolulu, Hawaii, traveled from coast to coast with this Liberty Bell replica to generate support for Hawaii statehood. Former President Truman graciously poses for a photograph with him at the Truman Library, July 28, 1958.

Greece long admired Harry Truman for coming to its defense against Communist rebels after World War II. Here a delegation of Greek officials meet with him in his office at the Truman Library, August 8, 1958.

In 1959, Truman agreed to make a few phone calls to help raise funds to restore the 100-year-old jail in Independence. His first call was to Joyce Hall of Hallmark in Kansas City to secure a $1,000 donation. The next three calls he made began, "This is Harry Truman . . ." and were met with "I'll bet!" and a hang-up on the other end.

To the dismay of Democrat leadership, Truman publicly and pointedly challenged John F. Kennedy's ability to run the country at such a young age. Ever smooth, Kennedy visited the former president at the Truman Library and the two made peace. Here Truman stumps for Kennedy as part of a nine-state, thirteen-speech tour in 1960.

Still "Captain Harry" to his men, Truman continued to attend reunions of the 35th Division into his later years. This one was held at the Muehlebach Hotel in Kansas City, around 1960.

Truman always enjoyed long car trips and as a senator often drove himself back and forth between Independence and Washington. In his lifetime he owned about a dozen Chrysler products. Here Charles Haines of the Haines-Hodges dealership hands over the keys to a new Chrysler New Yorker.

Throughout his political career, Truman never shied from giving tough-tongued advice. Here, at 75, he addresses students at the Truman Library in 1960. "I always tell students that it is what you learn after you know it all that counts," he said.

Visiting Margaret's family over Labor Day 1961, Harry and Bess took time out to attend a Yankees-Senators game in New York. Though Bess was the only real baseball fan in the family, Harry poses here with Roger Maris (left) and Mickey Mantle (right) during their momentous chase to break Babe Ruth's single-season home-run record.

Truman addresses the crowd at the Liberty Memorial in Kansas City on Armistice Day 1961. The big story of the day was the hatchet-burying between Truman and Eisenhower. Ike appeared at the Truman Library, stretched out his hand, and said, "How do you do, sir?" Truman shook Ike's hand and replied, "Won't you come in?"

In 1962 television producer David Susskind began taping a series of 13 one-hour documentaries about Truman's presidency, but the long-delayed series would not air until 1964 in 30-minute episodes. Truman was sometimes quite frank, even belligerent, but he was awarded "Outstanding Television Personality of the Year."

Seated at the same table on which the Truman Doctrine was signed, President Lyndon Johnson signs the Medicare bill at the Truman Library in 1965. Truman began the push for this legislation as president in 1945. Johnson remarked, "The people voted for Harry Truman not because he gave them hell—but because he gave them hope."

Margaret and Bess join Harry in receiving President Lyndon Johnson in the family home on October 11, 1968. Johnson stopped by Independence en route to his ranch in Texas to sign a proclamation acknowledging Truman's role in creating the United Nations and declaring October 24 United Nations Day.

Pat Nixon, Harry and Bess listen to President Richard Nixon play piano. Bitter enemies after Truman thought Nixon called him a traitor during the Red Scare, they did not make up, but were cordial. In 1960, Truman had told voters, "If you vote for Nixon, you ought to go to hell" and "He's never told the truth in his life."

Harry S. Truman died in a Kansas City hospital on December 26, 1972, at the age of 88. He had approved an elaborate funeral—a "fine show," he said—but Bess approved only a series of small rituals: an Episcopalian service, a Masonic rite, and a Baptist prayer. Here the Honor Guard watches over the former president's casket.

The line to say good-bye to Harry stretched half a mile through Independence. His final wishes were that he be buried in the courtyard of the Truman Library. "I want to be out there so I can get up and walk into my office if I want to." He received one final 21-gun salute and was buried December 28, 1972.

Notes on the Photographs

These notes, listed by page number, attempt to include all aspects known of the photographs. Each of the photographs is identified by the page number, photograph's title or description, photographer and collection, archive, and call or box number when applicable. Although every attempt was made to collect all available data, in some cases complete data was unavailable due to the age and condition of some of the photographs and records.

II **TRUMAN SIGNS CHECKS**
Courtesy of the Harry S.
Truman Library
64-1514

VI **RESERVES**
Courtesy of the Harry S.
Truman Library
58-479

X **CHRISTENING AND LAUNCHING OF THE USS MISSOURI**
Courtesy of the Harry S.
Truman Library
58-769-12

2 **WEDDING PHOTOGRAPH OF HARRY TRUMAN'S PARENTS**
Courtesy of the Harry S.
Truman Library
62-96

3 **HARRY S. TRUMAN, 1884**
Courtesy of the Harry S.
Truman Library
62-95

4 **PORTRAIT OF WILLIAM THOMAS TRUMAN**
Courtesy of the Harry S.
Truman Library
2006-71

5 **HARRY TRUMAN'S GRANDMOTHER**
Courtesy of the Harry S.
Truman Library
84-50

6 **909 WALDO, INDEPENDENCE, MISSOURI**
Courtesy of the Harry S.
Truman Library
84-62

7 **HARRY TRUMAN, AGE THIRTEEN**
Courtesy of the Harry S.
Truman Library
79-26

8 **MARY MARTHA (AUNT MATTIE) TRUMAN**
Courtesy of the Harry S.
Truman Library
2006-70

9 **SENIOR CLASS PHOTO, INDEPENDENCE HIGH SCHOOL, 1901**
Courtesy of the Harry S.
Truman Library
66-9984

10 **TRUMAN WITH RELATIVES**
Courtesy of the Harry S.
Truman Library
72-3615

11 **MARTHA ELLEN TRUMAN ON GRANDVIEW FARM**
Courtesy of the Harry S.
Truman Library
84-18

12 **NATIONAL GUARD UNIFORM**
Courtesy of the Harry S.
Truman Library
79-25

13 **TRUMAN AND WALLACES**
Courtesy of the Harry S.
Truman Library
82-58-13

14 **TRUMAN WITH FAMILY AT GRANDVIEW**
Courtesy of the Harry S.
Truman Library
77-3970

15 **TRUMAN IN BATTERY B UNIFORM**
Courtesy of the Harry S.
Truman Library
79-23

16 **HARRY S. TRUMAN**
Courtesy of the Harry S.
Truman Library
82-152

17 **ON THE FAMILY FARM**
Courtesy of the Harry S.
Truman Library
64-100

18 **IN FRONT OF RAILROAD TRAIN CAR**
Courtesy of the Harry S.
Truman Library
84-61

19 **BESS WALLACE TRUMAN AND HARRY ON A FISHING TRIP**
Courtesy of the Harry S.
Truman Library
84-80

20 **HARRY AND BESS IN CAR**
Courtesy of the Harry S.
Truman Library
84-37

21 **TRUMAN IN FRONT OF OIL WELL**
Courtesy of the Harry S.
Truman Library
82-58-79

22 **CONSISTORY OF WESTERN MISSOURI NO. 2**
Courtesy of the Harry S.
Truman Library
59-135

24 **BATTERY D, 129TH FIELD ARTILLERY**
Courtesy of the Harry S.
Truman Library
61-116-20